Enriched Language Arts - Term Paper – Steward

Research

1. Choose one reference from each categories:
   - Primary source – history/science textbook, professional article
   - Reference – print encyclopedia
   - Periodical – magazine, newspaper
     - No Internet sources at all
2. Make a bibliography card for each reference (3 total, minimum)
3. Make at least **6** note cards from each reference (18 total, minimum)

Writing the Paper

300-400 words (don't count articles: a, an, the) *everything must be typed*

max 475

1. Follow MLA format for all sections and area of the assignment
2. Typing paper, front of paper only *12pt times new roman black*
   - Double space
   - One-inch margins at both sides and bottom of paper
   - Indent first line of each paragraph
   - Last name and Page Numbers in upper right-hand corner
3. Works Cited (Bibliography) included as last (separate) page of paper
   - Three different (required types noted above) sources must be cited **within** paper

Dates Due

February 19 (Wednesday)
- Term paper title (question format) *topic*

February 26 (Wednesday)
- *hand out* Graphic Organizer Web
- 3 areas to be explored in paper *one sheet*
- Thesis Statement

March 5 *19* – (Wednesday)
- Three bibliography cards + one note card from each
  - 1 – primary source + 1 note card
  - 1 – periodical + 1 note card
  - 1 – print encyclopedia + 1 note card

March 19 *26* - (Wednesday)
- All 18 Notecards (6 note cards for each source – minimum)
- 3 - Bibliography Cards (1 per source type) *- with corrections*

March 26 - (Wednesday)
- Outline for term paper (MLA format) *April 2*

April 2 *9* - (Wednesday)
- Introductory and Conclusion paragraphs *16*

April 9 - (Wednesday)
- Rough draft - completed term paper with in-text citations and Works Cited page *23*

April 16 – (Wednesday) – 2 grades (one per rubric)
- Final Term Paper (meeting length specifications and rubric requirements)
- Works Cited page as the last page of paper (continuing the number in heading)

- Bibliography cards (3 sources, minimum: primary, reference, and periodical)
- 18 - Note cards (6 per source, minimum)
- ALL rough draft/edited items:
  - Rough Draft
  - Outline
  - Introductory paragraph
  - Conclusion paragraph

ORANGUTANS

Published by Creative Education, Inc., 123 South Broad Street, Mankato, Minnesota 56001

Library of Congress Cataloging-in-Publication Data

Wexo, John Bonnett.
Orangutans / by John Bonnett Wexo.
p.   cm. — (Zoobooks)
Originally published as an issue of Zoobooks: San Diego, CA, 1988.
Includes index.
Summary: Describes the physical characteristics, habitat, life cycle, and daily activities of this human-like animal.
ISBN 0-88682-412-5
1. Orangutan—Juvenile literature. [1. Orangutan.] I. Title. II. Series: Zoo books (Mankato, Minn.)
QL737.P96W39   1991   599.88'42—dc20   91-9947 CIP AC

ORANGUTANS

Created and Written by
John Bonnett Wexo

Zoological Consultant
Charles R. Schroeder, D.V.M.
Director Emeritus
San Diego Zoo &
San Diego Wild Animal Park

Scientific Consultants
Charles A. McLaughlin, Ph.D.
Mark Rich, M.S.

Creative Education

Photographic Credits

Front Cover: Zoological Society of San Diego; **Pages Six and Seven (background):** Tom McHugh (Photo Researchers); **Page Ten: Top,** M. Austerman (Animals Animals; **Bottom Left,** Tom McHugh, Monkey Jungle (Photo Researchers); **Bottom Right,** Los Angeles Zoo; **Page Eleven: Top Left,** C. McDougal (Ardea); **Top Right,** Tom McHugh (Photo Researchers); **Middle,** James M. Carmichael (Bruce Coleman); **Bottom,** Alice K. Taylor (Photo Researchers); **Pages Fourteen and Fifteen:** Kenneth Fink (Ardea); **Pages Sixteen and Seventeen: Left,** Rod Brindamour; **Right,** Charles Van Valkenburgh; **Page Eighteen: Top,** Tom McHugh (Photo Researchers); **Bottom Left,** Rod Brindamour; **Bottom Right,** Tom McHugh (Photo Researchers); **Page Nineteen: Top,** Los Angeles Zoo; **Middle Left,** Rod Brindamour; **Middle Right,** Tom McHugh (Photo Researchers); **Bottom Right,** M. Austerman (Animals Animals); **Pages Twenty and Twenty-One:** Rod Brindamour; **Page Twenty-Two and Inside Back Cover:** Rod Brindamour.

Art Credits

Paintings by Davis Meltzer

Our Thanks To: Charles L. Bieler; Richard L. Binford; Rod Brindamour; Ron Garrison; Andrew Grant; Joan Hallett; Susan Hathaway; Edalee Harwell; Richard Herczog; Marcia Hobbs; Thomas McArdle; William Noonan; John Ochse; Barbara Sallar; Dr. Warren Thomas; Carole Towne; Lynnette Wexo.

Special Thanks To: John W. Anderson

Contents

Bornean Male, over 15 years old

3 to 4 years old

Sumatran Male, over 15 years old

5 to 7 years old

Orangutan means "person of the forest" or "wild man." The name reveals the main reason why people have always found these great red apes interesting and mysterious. It is because orangs often look and act so much like human beings.

Orangutans are members of the same family as gorillas and chimpanzees. Smaller than gorillas, they are still very large for animals that spend most of their time living in trees. Males can be 4½ feet tall, and are often very

powerful. In the wild, they usually weigh about 160 pounds. Females are much smaller, with an average weight of 80 pounds. In the zoo, where more food is available, males can weigh over 350 pounds.

There are two different kinds of orangutans, which live on two separate islands in the country of Indonesia. On the island of Borneo, the orangs tend to be heavy-set, with coarse orange-red hair and dark grey skin. The hair is often very long on their shoulders

7 to 9 years old

Bornean Female, over 9 years old

6 to 12 months old

4 to 6 years old

Bornean Male, over 12 years old

and back. Sometimes it is more than a foot long. Males of the Borneo group develop huge cheek flaps as they grow older, as well as large pouches of pebbly skin that cover their chests.

Orangs from the island of Sumatra have narrower faces. They are usually taller than their Bornean relatives, and more slender. Their hair is also long, but lighter in color. Males of this group often have long flowing mustaches and beards that can make them look like wise old men.

In the wild, orangutans may live to be more than 40 years old. In the zoo, where medical care is available, they have been known to live for 57 years. Their intelligence can be amazing, and scientists believe that orangs are among the most intelligent of all land animals. As a group, they are famous for their skill in using their hands and simple tools. In zoos, they are known as "escape artists" who can find very clever ways to get out of their enclosures.

If you remove the hair of an orangutan, he looks very much like a person. But there are many differences between orangs and people.

An orangutan has a broader chest and narrower hips than a man of the same size.

Made for the High Life

Orangutans are superbly adapted for life in the trees. For most of them, the leafy canopy of the tropical forest provides everything they need in life, and they rarely descend to the forest floor.

One reason for the high life of an orangutan is safety. In the upper levels of the forest, they have no natural enemies. As they swing from tree to tree, the only danger they face is the possibility of a bone-breaking fall. At night, when predators prowl below, they sleep soundly in nests that they build as much as 70 feet up in the air.

The swing of an orang seems effortless. They move along through the trees by a process scientists call brachiation (BRAKE-EE-AY-SHUN). First they hook the fingers of one hand loosely over a branch and swing forward. Then the other hand is hooked loosely over the next branch, and so on.

The small body hangs from the long arms like the pendulum of a clock, and the length of the arm acts to propel the body forward with a minimum of work. The process seems

The arms of an orangutan are 1½ times longer than its legs. And they are much stronger than the legs.

The reach of orangutans is huge—as much as 8 feet from fingertip to fingertip. Their long arms can swing in all directions.

An orangutan can use both its hands and its feet to swing.

so easy and natural, but baby orangs are not born with the ability. Their mothers must patiently teach them how it is done.

The lighter an orangutan is, it seems, the more active and daring he is. Young orangs swing in the highest branches, scampering to the tops of the tallest trees to look around for food. As they grow older and heavier, their caution increases. Older orangs move slowly from branch to branch, often testing the strength of each new branch before putting their full weight on it.

The graceful acrobat of the treetops changes dramatically when he comes down to earth. On the ground, an orangutan's long arms get in his way. His short legs have trouble supporting the weight of his body. He must use his arms like crutches, planting them on the ground and swinging between them. Or he can stand up on his hind legs and waddle along, using his arms like the balancing poles of a wire walker. Not surprisingly, orangutans will usually go to great lengths to find a tree route when they want to go anywhere.

9

Every Orangutan is Unique

Orangutans display almost as much variety in their appearance as people do. The color and length of each one's hair is different. The shapes of their faces are different. And they have many different personalities. There is no doubt about it—orangs are individuals.

Different Bodies for Different Lives

The bodies of human beings are built for the kind of life that a human lives. The same is true for orangutans. Our first impression may be that orangs look a lot like us. But when you look closely, many important differences can be seen.

The human skeleton is made for life on the ground. The legs are longer and more powerful than the arms because they must carry the weight of the body. People stand upright because it is easier to walk that way.

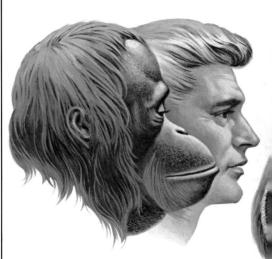

An orangutan's jaws are much larger than human jaws. They are very strong and have tremendous biting and crushing ability.

The hands of orangutans do not have the long, grasping thumbs that humans have. But orangutans are still very good with their hands. Some of them have learned to eat with spoons and forks, and to wash clothes in a bucket with soap and water.

An orangutan's prehensile feet are more practical up in the trees than human feet.

As male orangutans get older, they often grow beautiful beards. At first glance, these seem very much like human beards. But the texture and pattern of the hair is not the same.

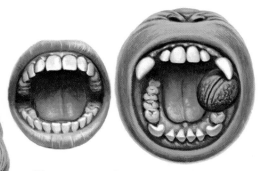

Human teeth are used for eating both plants and meat. Orangutan teeth are made for eating only plants. The heavy back teeth can crack even the hardest nuts. Like humans, orangutans have 32 teeth . . . and they get cavities.

The lips of orangutans play a major role in the animal's life. Orangutans will often "pucker up" to feel the texture of a piece of fruit before they bite into it. By pulling the lips way back and revealing his teeth, an orangutan makes it clear that he is angry. And the mouth is used just to carry things— often surprisingly large things.

The fingerprints of orangutans look a lot like human fingerprints. But orangutan fingers are more pointed.

The skeleton of an orangutan is similar in general form to a human skeleton, but the proportions are very different. The arms carry the weight of the animal, so they are long and strongly built. The legs do not carry weight very often, so they are short and less strongly built.

13

Eating is Everything

Food is the consuming passion of an orangutan's life. Every hour that an orang is awake, he is more likely to be looking for food than to be doing anything else. And this is only a matter of sheer necessity, because orangutans are the largest-bodied fruit-eating animals on earth. They simply have to eat a lot of fruit and other things to survive.

Everything in the life of a wild orangutan revolves around the search for food. Even the social structure of orangs in the forest is determined by the location and number of food sources. Fruit trees are usually widely separated, and there is rarely enough fruit on a single tree for more than one or two orangs to eat. As a result, male orangutans travel alone, and females are usually accompanied by only one or two of their own children.

Wild orangutans eat more than 300 kinds of foods. From April to November of each year, many different fruits ripen, and the animals eat heavily to build up a fat reserve. During the rest of the year, when fruit is scarce, the diet consists mostly of leaves, bark, and anything else that can be found.

In the zoo, every attempt is made to give orangutans the same kind of nourishment they get in the wild. But the kinds of foods that are served are not usually the same as wild orangs eat. A typical zoo diet could include apples, bananas, celery, sweet potatoes, milk, and monkey chow.

Orangs in zoos often have a weight problem. Unless the amount of food they get every day is controlled very carefully, they just keep eating and eating until they grow very fat. In the wild, their ability to build up a fat reserve is good, since it helps them get through the lean months of the year. But in the zoo, the same tendency to store fat can be harmful. Zoo keepers spend a great deal of time trying to keep orangutans satisfied without overfeeding them.

JACKFRUIT

DURIAN

LANGSAT

WILD PLUM

MANGOSTEEN

PITH OF WADAN,
OR CLIMBING BAMBOO

16

BREADFRUIT,
OR PANDANUS

RAMBUTAN

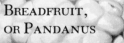

STRANGLING FIG

Eat-Wel

MONKEY FOOD

MILK MILK

RAISINS

What Mother Could Refuse Them Anything?

Young orangutans are very cute — and very spoiled. During the first four years of their lives, their mothers carry them almost everywhere. As they grow older, they become very active and develop a talent for "getting into things." But no matter what they do, they are seldom disciplined.

The Future of Orangutans is Up to Us...

Many people feel that orangutans will soon die out in the wild. Less than 2000 of them probably remain in Borneo, and the number in Sumatra is even smaller. As the human population of the islands increases, more and more forest is being cut down for lumber and to make room for farms. When the trees go, the orangutans go with them.

Another thing that works against the survival of wild orangs is their slow rate of reproduction. Orangutan mothers usually have only one baby at a time, and they may nurse them for as long as four years. Recent research has indicated that they may only have a baby every eight or nine years. The average female may only have two or three babies during her lifetime.

Fortunately, the Indonesian government has started to establish preserves to protect orangs. And scientists are now at work trying to find ways to increase the breeding success of the species in zoos. The zoo population of orangutans is steadily increasing, and there seems to be a good chance that these unique animals will at least survive in captivity. Orangutans are in trouble because people have destroyed their habitat—it is up to people to save them.

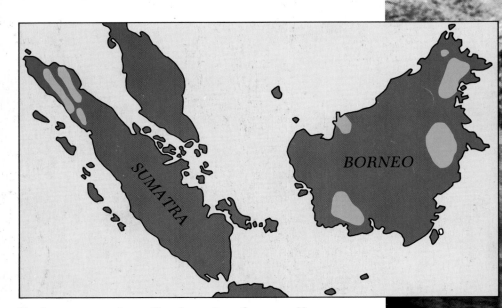

SUMATRA

BORNEO

Today, orangutans live in only a few small areas. If the trees in these areas are cut down, there will no longer be any place for them to live. In the future, orangutans may only survive in zoos.

22

Index